Contents

* easy

** medium

*** difficult

Words appearing in the text in bold, **like this**, are explained in the glossary.

Festival recipes

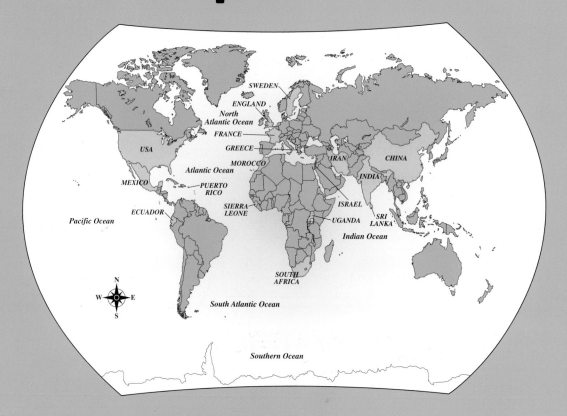

What is a festival?

A festival is a time when people celebrate to mark an important event. Whole families or groups of friends often eat together as part of the celebration. The food they eat will be something special – and usually there will be plenty of it.

Many of the special foods eaten at festivals are made using traditional recipes. The ones in this book are from the countries shown in yellow on the map above.

Festivals around the world

There are many different festivals celebrated all over the world. Some of the best-known festivals are linked to religions, such as Christmas and Easter for Christians.

Other festivals celebrate special days, such as New Year – but New Year may not always be 1 January.

Festival Foods

Jenny Vaughan and
Penny Beauchamp

www.heinemann.co.uk/library
Visit our website to find out more information about **Heinemann Library** books.

To order:
 Phone 44 (0) 1865 888066

Send a fax to 44 (0) 1865 314091

Visit the Heinemann Bookshop at www.heinemann.co.uk/library to browse our
catalogue and order online.

First published in Great Britain by Heinemann Library, Halley Court, Jordan Hill, Oxford OX2 8EJ, part of Harcourt Education.

Heinemann is a registered trademark of Harcourt Education Ltd.

Produced for Heinemann Library by Discovery Books Ltd.
Editorial: Helena Attlee, Geoff Barker, Nancy Dickmann and Tanvi Rai
Design: Jo Hinton-Malivoire and Rob Norridge
Illustrations: Nicholas Beresford-Davies
Cartographer: Stefan Chabluk
Picture Research: Laura Durman
Production: Séverine Ribierre

Originated by Dot Gradations Ltd.
Printed in China by WKT Company Limited

British Library Cataloguing in Publication Data
Vaughan, Jenny and Beauchamp, Penny
   Festival Foods. – (A world of recipes)
   641.5'67
A full catalogue record for this book is available from the British Library.

Acknowledgements
The Publishers would like to thank the following for permission to reproduce photographs: Patrick Ward/Corbis: p. **5**; Steve Lee: pp. **28, 29**; all other photographs by Terry Benson.

Cover photographs reproduced with permission of Terry Benson.

Our thanks to Sian Davies, home economist.

Disclaimer
All the Internet addresses (URLs) given in this book were valid at the time of going to press. However, due to the dynamic nature of the Internet, some addresses may have changed, or sites may have ceased to exist since publication. While the author and publishers regret any inconvenience this may cause readers, no responsibility for any such changes can be accepted by either the author or the publishers.

Every effort has been made to contact copyright holders of any material reproduced in this book. Any omissions will be rectified in subsequent printings if notice is given to the publishers.

The paper used to print this book comes from sustainable resources.

For example, the Chinese New Year falls in early spring, while in the Hindu religion, New Year falls in October or November, and is celebrated at the festival of *Divali* (see page 42). The Jewish New Year – *Rosh Hashanah* – also falls at around this time of the year.

Some festivals belong to only one town or village. Others may be celebrated in slightly varied ways, but in many different places at the same time. Family occasions, such as weddings or birthdays, are also festivals of a kind. There are thousands of festivals all over the world, with an enormous variety of foods that are prepared especially for them.

Fasts

A fast is the opposite of a festival – a more solemn time, when people give up certain foods, or even all food, depending on their religion or custom. During Lent, many

Women carrying offerings of food during a festival in Bali, Indonesia.

Christians do not eat meat or rich foods until the great celebration of Easter. Muslims keep to a fast that lasts throughout Ramadan – the ninth month of the Islamic year. At this time, Muslims may not eat or drink between sunrise and sunset. Ramadan ends with a festival called *Eid-ul-Fitr* during which special foods are eaten. Many fasting periods either begin or end with a special meal.

5

Ingredients

fresh thyme

chillies

fresh ginger

dried oregano

cinnamon

bay leaves

cumin

saffron

cardamom pods

Special foods

Festivals are special party times, and the food that goes with them is special, too. Festival recipes often include food that used to be too expensive for people to eat very often.

Spices

Spices used to be very expensive because in many parts of the world they had to be transported for hundreds of kilometres across the sea. They were only used to give food a unique taste on a really important occasion, such as a festival. Some spices, like cumin or cardamom, are sold as seeds or pods. They can also be ground up to make a powder. Cinnamon is sold in sticks made from the bark of a tree. All spices have quite a strong flavour, so you do not need to use very much of them.

Saffron

One of the most expensive spices is saffron. It is made from the orange-coloured **stigmas** inside a special kind of crocus flower. Luckily, you will only ever need it in tiny amounts. If you cannot get saffron, use a drop or two of yellow food colouring instead. This will not flavour the food, but it will give you the right yellow colour.

Ginger

Ginger is a spicy root that can be used in both sweet and savoury dishes. Some of the recipes in this book use fresh ginger. This is a root that must be **peeled** and either finely **chopped** or **grated** before it is used. Other recipes require ginger that has been dried and ground into a powder.

Chillies

A dish that contains chilli peppers will always taste hot. Chillies come in a variety of colours and sizes. Some are extremely hot while others have a much milder flavour. Always be very careful when you are handling chillies. Never rub your eyes or nose, as the chilli oil left on your fingers will make them sting.

Herbs

Herbs are used to add a delicious flavour to food. Thyme is a Mediterranean herb that thrives in hot, dry conditions. Like most other herbs, it can be used either fresh or dried. When herbs are dried it often makes their flavour stronger. Dried oregano is frequently **sprinkled** over pizzas in Italy. Bay leaves tend to be used to flavour soups and stews. In the past, people would only have used the herbs that they could pick near their homes, but today we can buy fresh or dried herbs from all over the world.

Before you start

Kitchen rules

There are a few basic rules you should always follow when you are cooking.

- Ask an adult if you can use the kitchen.
- Some cooking processes, especially **frying**, and those using **boiling** water or syrup, can be dangerous. When you see this sign, always ask an adult to help you.
- Wipe down any work surfaces before you start cooking, and then wash your hands.
- Wear an apron to protect your clothes, and tie back long hair.
- Be very careful when using sharp knives.
- Never leave pan handles sticking out, because you might knock the pan over.
- Always wear oven gloves to lift things in and out of the oven.
- Wash fruit and vegetables before you use them.

How long will it take?

Some of the recipes in this book are very quick and easy to make, while others are more difficult and may take much longer. The strip across the top of the right-hand page of each recipe tells you how long it will take to make each dish. It also shows you how difficult the dish is to make: every recipe is either * (easy), ** (medium) or *** (quite difficult). Why not start with the easier recipes?

Quantities and measurements

You can see how many people each recipe will serve by looking at the strip across the top of the right-hand page. You can multiply the quantities if you are cooking for more people. Avoid changing the quantities of ingredients in a cake or a loaf, as this will alter the time that it takes to **bake**.

Ingredients in recipes can be measured in two different ways. Metric measurements use grams, litres and millilitres. Imperial measurements use ounces and fluid ounces. This book uses metric measurements. If you want to convert them into imperial measurements, use the chart on page 44.

In the recipes, you will see the following abbreviations:
tbsp = tablespoon   g = grams   kg = kilograms
tsp = teaspoon   ml = millilitres   cm = centimetres

Utensils

To cook the recipes in this book you will need these utensils (as well as essentials, such as spoons, plates and bowls):

- baking foil
- baking tray
- **baking parchment**
- cake rack
- **chopping** board
- **colander**
- **draining** spoon
- large dried beans
- **fish slice**
- food processor or blender
- frying pan (with a lid)
- **grater**
- measuring jug
- round flan tin (20cm, non-stick)
- omelette pan (non-stick)
- **ovenproof** dish about 16 x 23cm
- pastry brush
- rolling pin and a pastry board
- 2-litre saucepan
- smaller non-stick saucepans
- set of scales
- sieve
- square and round cake tins (20cm, non-stick)
- sharp knife
- **whisk**

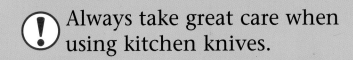 Always take great care when using kitchen knives.

Savoury dumplings (China)

Dumplings are often served during the festivities that mark the Chinese New Year. Nobody does any work during the festival, and so food is prepared in advance to be eaten later.

What you need

1 spring onion
fresh ginger root,
  about 1cm long
300g *pak choi*, or
  Chinese leaves
250g minced pork
1 tbsp soy sauce
175g plain flour

What you do

1 Wash the spring onion, cut off the root and **chop** finely.

(!) 2 **Peel** and chop the ginger root very finely.

3 Chop the *pak choi* or Chinese leaves very finely.

(!) 4 Bring a pan of water to the **boil**. Add the *pak choi* and boil for 3 minutes. **Drain** the leaves through a sieve, **rinse** them under a cold tap and spread them out on kitchen paper.

5 Thoroughly mix the **minced** pork, spring onion and *pak choi*, ginger and **soy sauce** together. Wash your hands.

6 Put the flour in a bowl and make a **well** in the middle. Gradually add 115ml water, stirring all the time with a fork to make a sticky **dough**.

7 **Knead** the dough on a floured board for 5–10 minutes, until it is smooth and stretchy. Roll it into a sausage shape with your hands.

8 Cut the dough into 16 equal pieces and then roll out each one to make a thin circle. Place a teaspoonful of filling on each circle.

9 Fold each circle in half, pressing the sides firmly together and then use a fork to seal the edges.

(!) 10 Bring a large pan of water to the boil. Drop 2 or 3 dumplings into it and cook them for 20 minutes. Take them out with a draining spoon.

11 Cook the rest of the dumplings in batches of 2 or 3. If you put too many in the pan they will begin to stick together. Serve with soy sauce.

Pescado en escabeche (Puerto Rico)

Puerto Rico is an island in the Caribbean which lies between the continents of North and South America. This recipe is made during the Christian Holy Week – the week before Easter.

What you need

400g cod, haddock or
  hake, with bones
  removed
30g flour
¼ tsp paprika
60ml olive oil
¼ mild onion
small garlic clove
6 peppercorns
1 large bay leaf
salt and pepper
30ml white wine vinegar

What you do

1 Cut the fish into 4 pieces.

2 Place the fish pieces on a plate and **sift** the flour on to them. Make sure they are all covered with flour.

3 **Sprinkle** the fish with paprika.

4 Heat 2 tbsp of olive oil in a **frying** pan and fry the fish in it, piece by piece, for 4 minutes on each side. Don't cook the fish too much, or it will start to fall apart when you lift it from the pan. Use a **fish slice** to remove the fish from the pan.

5 Allow the fish to dry on kitchen paper.

(!) **6** **Slice** the onion and garlic thinly.

7 Put the fish pieces in the bottom of a shallow dish that measures about 16 x 23cm. Scatter the onion, garlic and peppercorns on top. Break the bay leaf into 2 or 3 pieces and place them among the fish.

8 Sprinkle salt and pepper over the fish and vegetables.

9 **Whisk** the rest of the oil with the vinegar and pour it over the fish. Cover the dish and keep it in the fridge until you are ready to serve it, **basting** the fish from time to time with the oil and vinegar. This dish is delicious served with cold rice salad.

Ramadan soup (Morocco)

This dish, which is called *harira* in Morocco, is a cross between a soup and a stew. It is made during Ramadan, a fast that lasts for the whole of the ninth month of the Muslim year. Muslims do not eat or drink between sunrise and sunset during Ramadan, and *harira* makes a nourishing meal that is especially welcome at the end of a day of fasting.

What you need

200g lean lamb
1 onion
115g tinned chickpeas, **drained**
2 tbsp olive oil
400g tinned, chopped tomatoes, including their juice
115g dried red lentils
60g long-grain rice
1 tbsp tomato purée
¼ red pepper, chopped
juice of 1 lemon
1 tbsp chopped fresh coriander, or fresh coriander and parsley mixed

What you do

1 **Chop** the lamb into pieces of 2 x 2cm or less.

2 **Peel** and **slice** the onion.

3 **Rinse** the chickpeas.

(!) 4 Heat the oil in a large pan and **fry** the lamb for about 5 minutes, until it is lightly browned on all sides.

5 Add the onion and cook gently. When it is soft, add all the other ingredients except the fresh herbs.

(!) 6 Add 1 litre of water and bring the soup to the **boil**. **Simmer** for about 30 minutes, until the rice and lentils are cooked through.

7 Add the coriander, or the fresh herb mixture, and simmer for another 5 minutes. Serve hot.

New Year omelette (Iran)

This omelette recipe is from ancient Persia, the country that is now called Iran. It is made for a New Year festival that dates back to the time before Iran became an Islamic country, over 1000 years ago. Persian omelettes are unusual because, unlike the French omelettes that we are all used to, they are frequently **baked** in the oven, instead of being **fried** in a pan.

What you need

2 spring onions
1 leek
40g fresh spinach
  leaves
1 sprig parsley
1 tbsp fresh oregano
  and fresh thyme,
  mixed
6 large eggs
salt and black pepper
25g butter

What you do

1 **Preheat** the oven to 170°C/325°F/gas mark 3.

2 Wash all the vegetables and dry them on kitchen paper.

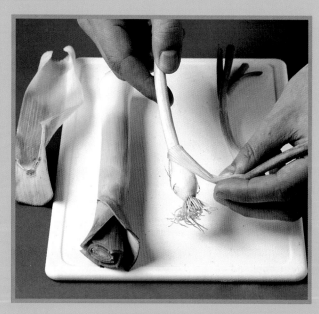

3 Remove any damaged outer leaves from the spring onions and leek. Cut off the root and green shoots.

4 **Chop** the spring onions, leek, spinach and herbs very finely.

5 **Beat** the eggs in a large bowl.

6 Mix in the vegetables. **Season** with salt and pepper.

7 **Grease** an **ovenproof** dish with butter. The exact size of the dish is not important, but it should be about 20cm across. A round, non-stick cake tin is ideal.

8 Pour the egg mixture into the dish and cover it with foil.

(!) 9 Bake for 30 minutes, and then remove the foil. Cook for another 10 minutes, until the egg has set and the mixture is brown on top.

Fanesca (Ecuador)

This soup is eaten during Lent in the South American country of Ecuador, where many people are Roman Catholics. Many Catholics do not eat meat during Lent, and so this fish recipe is very popular. Dried salt cod – called *bacalao* – is traditionally used in this dish. It can be hard to find, so we suggest using fresh cod or haddock in this extra tasty version.

What you need

1 onion
1 garlic clove
25g butter
1 tsp dried oregano
1 tsp ground cumin
salt and freshly ground
   black pepper
100g long-grain rice
250g mixed, frozen
   broad beans,
   sweetcorn, runner
   beans and peas
500ml vegetable stock
2 level tbsp cornflour
350ml milk
175g skinless cod or
   haddock fillet

What you do

1 **Peel** the onion and **slice** it finely.

2 Peel the garlic clove and **chop** it finely.

(!) 3 **Melt** the butter in a large saucepan and **fry** the onion and garlic over a low heat until the onion is soft, but not brown. This will take about 5 minutes.

(!) 4 Add the oregano, cumin, salt, pepper, rice, frozen vegetables and stock. Bring to the **boil**. Reduce the heat and **simmer** gently for about 30 minutes.

5 In a small jug or cup, blend the cornflour with 4 tbsp milk. Then add the remaining milk.

6 Cut the cod or haddock fillet into chunks and add them to the saucepan. Cook gently for about 4 minutes.

7 Stir the cornflour mixture to make sure that it is smooth, then add it to the saucepan, stirring all the time. Cook, stirring, for about 3 minutes, until the mixture thickens.

8 Ladle the soup into bowls and serve at once.

ADDED EXTRAS

In Ecuador, the soup is served with chopped, hard-boiled eggs, **grated** cheese, chopped peanuts and chopped parsley on top – so you can do this too, if you like.

Jolloff rice (Sierra Leone)

This popular party dish is cooked throughout West Africa. It is often served at the festive meal following a wedding, or on other important, family occasions such as birthday parties. People adapt the recipe according to the number of guests they are entertaining. Add more rice to make the food go further.

What you need

1 large onion
1 red chilli (not too hot)
100ml groundnut oil
   (or palm oil if you
   can get it)
500g chicken pieces,
   stewing beef or lamb
2 tbsp tomato purée
1 tsp fresh thyme or a
   large pinch of dried
   thyme
salt and pepper
100g long-grain rice

What you do

1 **Peel** and **slice** the onion finely.

2 Cut the chilli in half lengthways, remove the seeds and then **chop** it. Always wash your hands after you have handled chillies. Never touch your eyes when handling chillies.

3 Heat the oil in a saucepan. Add a little of the chicken or meat and **fry** it for a few minutes, until brown on all sides.

4 Take the meat out of the pan, put it into a warm dish, and fry the rest of the meat, in batches, until it is all browned. It does not have to be cooked right through. Set aside and keep warm.

(!) 5 Put the onion and chilli into the pan that you used for the meat. Fry over a low heat for about 10 minutes.

(!) 6 Add the tomato **purée**, thyme, salt and pepper, and about 100ml of water. Allow the mixture to **boil**.

7 Return the meat to the pan and **simmer** for about 20 minutes, or until the meat is **tender**. You may need to add a bit more water from time to time.

8 Add the rice and 200ml of water to the stew. Let it simmer for about 15 minutes, stirring all the time. Add a little more water if it seems to be drying out. Once the rice is cooked, the dish is ready to serve.

Makaronada (Greece)

This is a Greek version of macaroni cheese. Like Roman Catholics, members of the Greek Orthodox Church often avoid meat during the fast of Lent – the time when Christians remember the story of how Jesus spent 40 days fasting in the wilderness.

What you need

300ml milk
50g butter
100g plain white flour
3 eggs
125g macaroni
salt and pepper
125g Cheddar cheese

What you do

1 Warm the milk, but do not let it **boil**.

2 **Melt** the butter in another saucepan.

3 Add the flour to the melted butter a little at a time, stirring all the time. Keep the heat under the saucepan low.

4 Add the milk to the flour and butter mixture, a little at a time. Keep stirring so that there are no lumps. When the sauce is thick and creamy, let it cool.

5 Break 2 of the eggs into a bowl. Using a spoon, lift out the yolks. Mix them into the sauce, along with the other, whole egg. You do not need the spare egg whites in this recipe.

6 **Preheat** the oven to 220°C/425°F/gas mark 7.

7 Bring a large pan of water to the boil, add the macaroni and cook it until it is soft. This will take about 10 minutes.

(!) **8** Carefully **drain** the macaroni and add it to the sauce. **Season** with salt and pepper.

9 Put half the macaroni and sauce in an ovenproof dish of about 16 x 23cm.

10 **Grate** the cheese. Spread half of the grated cheese over the macaroni. Spoon the rest of the macaroni and sauce over it and then **sprinkle** the top with the remaining cheese.

(!) **11** **Bake** for about 20 minutes, until the surface of the makaronada is golden.

WHITE SAUCE

The flour-and-milk sauce is usually known by its French name, which is béchamel sauce. If lumps form (they often do), push the sauce through a sieve, whizz it in a blender, or **whisk** it with an electric whisk. Do this before adding the eggs. If the sauce is too thick, just add more milk.

Peanut sauce for chicken (Uganda)

This sauce is eaten with roast chicken on special occasions, such as birthday parties, wedding banquets or other family celebrations. The recipe makes enough sauce for a 1.5kg chicken. In Africa it is often made with freshly roasted and ground peanuts. Always check that none of your guests are allergic to nuts.

What you need

1 large onion
2 tbsp vegetable oil
227g tin chopped tomatoes (with their juice)
4 tbsp crunchy peanut butter
240ml milk
salt and pepper
1.5kg roast chicken, sliced

What you do

(!) **1** **Peel** and **chop** the onion finely.

(!) **2** Heat the oil in a large saucepan and **fry** the onion until it is golden.

3 Add the tomatoes, peanut butter, milk and a pinch of salt and pepper. Stir everything together.

4 Cover with a lid and **simmer** for about 20 minutes.

5 Check the sauce regularly, and stir it to make sure that it doesn't burn. Add a little water if the sauce seems to be getting too dry.

6 Serve the warm sauce with **slices** of roast chicken.

Mancha manteles (Mexico)

Mancha manteles is a Mexican dish and its name means 'table-cloth stainer' – you will see why when you try serving it! It is made in midsummer, when Christians remember the importance of the Holy Communion or Mass during the Festival of Corpus Christi.

What you need

400g lean pork fillets
2 tbsp vegetable oil
400g chicken pieces
4 mild chillies
½ red pepper
30g flaked almonds
1 tbsp sesame seeds
1 tbsp white wine vinegar
200g tinned tomatoes
1 cinnamon stick
2 eating apples
1 unripe or nearly ripe banana
140g **drained** tinned, unsweetened pineapple

What you do

1 Cut the pork into 4 pieces.

(!) 2 Heat 200ml water in a pan, and then add the pork and let it cook gently.

(!) 3 Meanwhile, heat the oil in a **frying** pan and fry the chicken until it is brown on all sides, but not cooked through.

4 Add the chicken to the saucepan with the pork. Keep the oil in the frying pan as you will use it again later.

(!) 5 Cut the chillies in half lengthways, remove the seeds and then **chop** them finely. Always wash your hands after you have handled chillies. Never touch your eyes when handling chillies.

6 Remove the seeds from the pepper and chop it into small pieces.

7 Put the almonds, sesame seeds, chillies and red pepper in the frying pan and fry them, stirring all the time, until the almonds are just turning brown.

8 Add the vinegar and tomatoes to the frying pan. Cook for another 3 minutes before putting the red pepper mixture into the saucepan with the chicken and pork.

9 Add the cinnamon stick, and enough water to almost cover the mixture.

(!) **10** **Peel** and chop the apples and banana, removing the apple core. Fry the fruit in oil for a few minutes and then add the pineapple.

11 Put the cooked fruit in the pan with the chicken and pork. Cover with a lid and **simmer** for 30 minutes. Remove the cinnamon stick before serving.

Pumpkin pie (USA)

Americans make this sweet, spiced pie to celebrate Thanksgiving. This festival dates back to 1621, when the early settlers in New England brought in the first harvest in their new country.

What you need

1 tbsp plain flour
300g ready-made **shortcrust** pastry
1kg fresh pumpkin
80ml milk
3 eggs
125g caster sugar
½ tsp ground nutmeg
½ tsp ground ginger
½ tsp ground cinnamon

What you do

1 Preheat the oven to 190°C/375°F/gas mark 5.

2 Sprinkle flour over a clean work surface. Roll out the pastry until you have a circle about 30cm wide.

3 Use the pastry to line a 20cm, round flan tin. Prick the base of the pastry case with a fork.

4 Put a 30cm square of **baking parchment** into the pastry case. Fill it with any large, dried beans. This will stop the pastry from puffing up in the oven.

(!) **5** Put the tin in the oven and **bake** the pastry for about 15 minutes. Then remove the beans and paper.

6 Cut the pumpkin into segments, remove the peel and seeds, **chop** and **rinse** 500g of the flesh.

(!) **7** Place the prepared pumpkin in a covered **colander** over a pan of **boiling** water and **steam** it for about 20 minutes, until it is very soft.

8 Put the pumpkin in a bowl with the milk and mash it. Let it **cool**.

9 **Whisk** the eggs, sugar, nutmeg, ginger and cinnamon together, and mix them into the pumpkin.

(!) 10 Spread the pumpkin mixture into the flan case. Bake it for about 40 minutes, or until filling has set. Serve hot or cold with whipped cream or vanilla ice-cream.

TINNED PUMPKIN

You can use a 500g tin of pumpkin instead of fresh pumpkin in this recipe. If you do use tinned pumpkin, you can leave out steps 6–8 in the recipe.

Tamil rice harvest pudding (Sri Lanka)

This dish is made by the Tamil people of Sri Lanka, to celebrate the rice harvest. Traditionally, it is made only from the purest white rice and fresh milk, as the pudding is an offering to the gods. It is cooked in a special pot, early in the morning, so that the first rays of the sun will strike the milk as it begins to boil.

What you need

600ml full cream milk
125g long-grain rice
1 short stick of
  cinnamon
pinch of crushed
  cardamom seeds
1 ripe banana
handful of raisins, dates
  or sultanas (or a
  mixture of all 3 fruits)
60g soft brown sugar

What you do

1 Put the milk in a non-stick saucepan.

(!) 2 Add the rice, cinnamon and cardamom and place it over a low heat. Bring it to the **boil**.

3 Let the rice **simmer** for an hour. Stir gently so that no rice grains stick to the bottom of the pan and burn.

4 When the rice has **absorbed** all the milk, check to see that it is cooked. Do this by testing 1 or 2 grains to see if they are soft all the way through. If the rice is not ready, add a little more milk and simmer for a little longer.

5 **Peel** and **slice** the banana. Add it to the rice, with the dried fruit and the sugar and stir well.

6 Leave the pudding off the heat for about 20 minutes, stirring it every now and again to stop a skin forming on top. This delicious pudding can be eaten hot or cold.

Crêpes (France)

The Christian fast of Lent starts on a Wednesday. The day before is called Shrove Tuesday. Traditionally, people used up all the rich foods in their larders on Shrove Tuesday, before the Lenten fast began the next day. This is why Shrove Tuesday is called *Mardi Gras*, (or fat Tuesday), in France. Pancakes, or *crêpes*, were a convenient way of using up eggs and milk or cream.

What you need

250g plain flour
pinch of salt
2 eggs
60g butter
500ml milk

What you do

1 In a mixing bowl, mix the flour and salt together.

2 Break the eggs into another bowl and **beat** them well.

(!) 3 **Melt** the butter in a **frying** pan.

4 Make a **well** in the flour and tip the beaten eggs into it.

5 Add the milk and about two-thirds of the melted butter. Leave the rest of the fat for frying the crêpes.

6 Beat all the mixture together to make a smooth **batter**. Let this stand for about an hour.

7 Add a little of the remaining melted butter to the base of a non-stick omelette pan and then place the pan over a gentle heat.

(!)8 When the butter starts to smoke, add a spoonful of crêpe mixture to the pan. Tip the pan from side to side, so that as much of the base as possible is covered by the mixture. Cook for about a minute, until the crêpe bubbles, and then use a non-stick **fish slice** to flip the crêpe over and cook the other side.

9 Slide the crêpe on to a warm plate and cover it with greaseproof paper while you make the rest of the crêpes, one at a time.

TASTY FILLINGS

For a savoury meal, make a filling for your crêpe using mushrooms, cheese or ham. For sweet pancakes, try fresh lemon juice and sugar, or jam and cream.

Santa Lucia cakes (Sweden)

Swedish girls serve these special cakes on Santa Lucia's day, 13 December. Saint Lucia was an early Christian. Many of her fellow Christians went into hiding because the Romans wanted to punish them for their faith. She bravely took food to them.

What you need

75g butter
2 pinches of saffron
300ml milk, plus 3 tbsp
700g strong bread flour
7g dried 'easy-blend' yeast (usually, this means 1 sachet)
115g granulated sugar
pinch of salt
2 beaten eggs
handful of raisins

What you do

1 **Melt** the butter gently in a small pan.

2 Put the saffron in 300ml of milk in another pan and warm it until it is **tepid**.

3 Mix the flour, **yeast**, sugar and salt in a warm bowl, and make a **well** in the centre.

4 Pour in the warm milk and saffron, the melted butter and 1 **beaten** egg into the well and stir.

5 **Knead** the **dough** on a floured board for about 10 minutes. Add more flour to the mixture if the dough becomes too sticky.

6 Put the dough in a warm place and cover it with cling-film. Leave for about 90 minutes to rise (grow) to twice its original size.

7 Add the raisins and knead the dough again. Divide into 24 evenly-sized pieces. Roll each into a sausage shape.

8 Cover a baking tray with **baking parchment**. Put the shapes on this, curling them to make 'S' or 'C' shapes. Leave them to rise for another 30 minutes.

9 **Preheat** the oven to 220°C/425°F/gas mark 7. Make a **glaze** by mixing 3 tbsp of milk with the other beaten egg. Let it stand for 5 minutes, then brush it over the buns.

10 **Bake** the buns for around 10 minutes, until they are golden brown. **Cool** them on a cake rack.

Parkin (England)

This ginger cake is eaten in England at Bonfire Night parties on 5 November. The celebration reminds people about Guy Fawkes, a man who took part in a plot to blow up King James I and the Houses of Parliament on 5 November 1605. He was caught, but people have always remembered the story by building bonfires and letting off fireworks.

What you need

50g butter
150g golden syrup
100g treacle
200g plain flour
250g medium oatmeal
50g granulated sugar
2 tsp ground ginger
1 egg, **beaten**
1 tsp bicarbonate of soda
2 tbsp milk

What you do

1 **Preheat** the oven to 170°C/325°F/gas mark 3.

2 **Grease** a non-stick, square cake tin, around 20 x 20cm with a little butter.

(!) **3** Gently, **melt** the butter, golden syrup and treacle together in a large saucepan, until they are runny. Allow the mixture to **cool** a little.

4 Stir in the flour, oatmeal, sugar, ginger and egg.

5 Mix the bicarbonate of soda and milk, and add them to the mixture.

(!) **6** Pour the mixture into the cake tin and **bake** it for about 50 minutes.

7 Turn the oven off, keep the door closed, and leave for a further 35 minutes. The parkin will sink a little in the middle of the tin.

8 Cut the parkin into equal squares as soon as it is cool enough to eat.

Cape Malay milk tart (South Africa)

This recipe is Malayan in origin, but it is made by Malay families who live in South Africa. There it is a traditional dish served at family weddings. The tart can be eaten either warm or cold, whichever you prefer.

What you need

1 tbsp plain flour
300g ready-made **shortcrust** pastry
500ml milk
1 tsp vanilla extract
50g plain flour
pinch of ground cinnamon (optional)
2 eggs
60g sugar

What you do

1 **Preheat** the oven to 170°C/325°F/gas mark 3.

2 **Sprinkle** 1 tbsp plain flour on a work surface and roll out the pastry to make a circle about 35cm across.

3 Use the pastry to line a non-stick flan dish of about 20cm in diameter. Trim off the extra pastry and prick the base of the pastry case with a fork.

4 Put a 30cm square of **baking parchment** into the pastry case. Fill it with any large, dried beans. This will stop the pastry from puffing up in the oven.

(!) 5 Put the tin in the oven and **bake** the pastry for about 15 minutes. Remove the beans and paper.

(!) 6 Warm the milk in a non-stick pan and add the vanilla **extract**.

7 In another non-stick pan, mix the flour with a little of the milk and vanilla mixture, stirring all the time, until you have a smooth **paste**.

(!) 8 Gently heat this paste, adding the warm milk a little at a time and stirring it so that no lumps form. When all the milk has been added, add the cinnamon if you are using it.

9 Let the sauce **simmer**, stirring until it thickens. This should take about 5 minutes. Let it **cool**.

10 **Beat** the eggs with the sugar, and gradually add them to the milk sauce mixture, stirring all the time.

11 Pour the milk sauce mixture into the pastry case and bake for about 25 minutes.

Honey cake (Israel)

This honey cake is made for *Rosh Hashanah*, a festival that falls in autumn and marks the beginning of the Jewish New Year. It is traditional to eat certain foods at this time, and this is one of them.

What you need

200g plain flour
pinch of salt
1½ tsp baking powder
1 tsp mixed spice
50g granulated sugar
4 eggs
250ml runny honey
75ml vegetable oil
1 tsp instant coffee
   dissolved in 100ml
   hot water
80g walnuts or almonds

What you do

1 **Preheat** the oven to 170°C/325°F/gas mark 3.

2 Mix flour, salt, baking powder and mixed spice in a large bowl.

3 **Whisk** the sugar and eggs together until they are thick and light-coloured.

4 Whisk in the honey, oil and coffee.

5 Add this mixture and the nuts to the flour mixture.

6 **Grease** a 20cm round cake tin with a little butter, and then pour the mixture into it. **Bake** for about 1 hour. Towards the end of that time, check that the cake is not getting too brown around the edges. If it is, turn the oven down and cover the cake with foil until it is cooked.

7 You can check if the cake is cooked by pushing a skewer or a knife into its centre. If the skewer comes out sticky, the cake is not quite done, but if it is clean, the cake is ready to come out of the oven.

8 Let the cake **cool** in its tin for about 15 minutes, and then turn it out on to a cake rack to cool completely.

Burfi (India)

Divali – the Hindu festival of light – takes place in the autumn. People decorate their homes and the streets with lights, have firework displays and share a family celebration. Indian-style sweets – called *burfi* – are a favourite at Hindu festivals. This is a simple recipe for coconut *burfi*.

What you need

200g creamed coconut
40g butter
1 tsp cardamom powder
a few strands of saffron
   (optional)
150g caster sugar
2 tbsp flaked almonds

What you do

1 Put the creamed coconut in a bowl over a pan of water.

2 Add half the butter, cardamom, saffron and sugar.

3 Place the pan over a very low heat and allow the creamed coconut and butter to **melt**.

4 Keep this mixture over the heat for 10 minutes, stirring it all the time.

5 Melt the remaining butter in a small pan. **Grease** a shallow dish, such as a 20cm square cake tin, with a little of the butter.

6 Pour the mixture into the greased cake tin and **sprinkle** almonds over it.

7 Allow the *burfi* to **cool**, and then cut it into small pieces.

Further information

Books

Festivals of the World, Professor Martin E. Marty (ed.)
(Hodder Wayland, 2002)
Sacred Food, Elizabeth Luard (MQ Publications, 2001)

Websites

http://kid.allrecipes.com
http://www.support4learning.org.uk/shap/calend2a.htm

Conversion chart

Ingredients for recipes can be measured in two different ways. Metric measurements use grams and millilitres. Imperial measurements use ounces and fluid ounces. This book uses metric measurements. The chart here shows you how to convert measurements from metric to imperial.

SOLIDS		LIQUIDS	
METRIC	IMPERIAL	METRIC	IMPERIAL
10g	¼ oz	30ml	1 fl oz
15g	½ oz	50ml	2 fl oz
25g	1 oz	75ml	2½ fl oz
50g	1¾ oz	100ml	3½ fl oz
75g	2¾ oz	125ml	4 fl oz
100g	3½ oz	150ml	5 fl oz
150g	5 oz	300ml	10 fl oz
250g	9 oz	600ml	20 fl oz
450g	1lb	900ml	30 fl oz

Healthy eating

This diagram shows you what foods you should eat to stay healthy. Most of your food should come from the bottom of the pyramid. Eat some of the foods from the middle every day. Only eat a little of the foods from the top.

Healthy eating at festival time

Festival foods are made to be eaten on very special occasions. Many of the recipes contain large quantities of sugar and fat. You should take care not to eat too much of these foods at one time, or to make them too often.

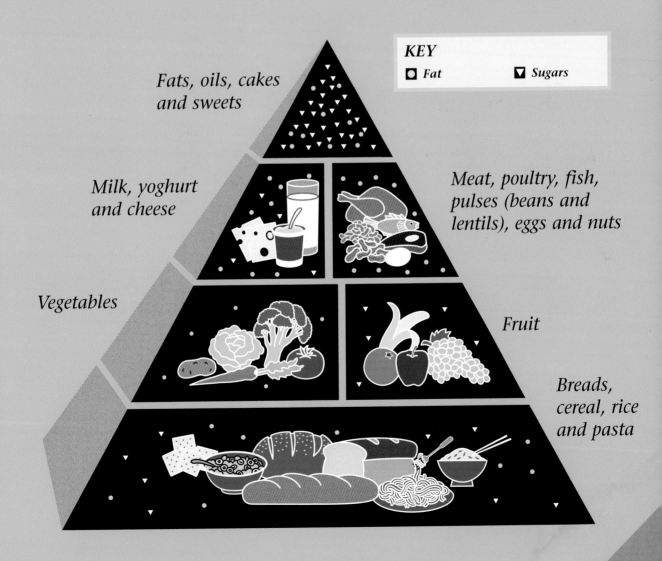

Fats, oils, cakes and sweets

KEY
◻ Fat ▼ Sugars

Milk, yoghurt and cheese

Meat, poultry, fish, pulses (beans and lentils), eggs and nuts

Vegetables

Fruit

Breads, cereal, rice and pasta

Glossary

absorb soak up

bake cook something, such as cakes or pies, in the oven

baking parchment paper with a non-stick surface that can be used to line baking trays or cake tins

baste spoon fat or oil over food to stop it drying out

batter a beaten mixture of flour, eggs and milk, for instance, that is used for making pancakes

beat mix something together strongly, using a fork, spoon or whisk

boil cook a liquid on the hob (or the flat top part of the cooker). Boiling liquid bubbles and steams strongly.

chop cut something into pieces, using a knife

colander bowl-shaped container with holes in it, used for straining vegetables and draining

cool allow hot food to become cold. You should always allow food to cool before putting it in the fridge.

dough a soft mixture that sticks together and can be shaped or rolled out – not too wet to handle, but not dry either

drain allow liquid to run out or away. A draining spoon is a large spoon with holes in its bowl.

extract flavouring, such as vanilla or almond extract. It is not the same as essence, which is much stronger.

fish slice utensil for lifting fish or other fried food out of a pan. It is like a flat spoon with slits in it.

fry cook something in oil in a pan

glaze coat food with liquid, such as a mixture of milk and egg; used to make top of bread or buns glossy during baking

grate cut into small pieces, using a grater (a kitchen utensil with lots of small holes)

grease rub fat over a surface to stop food sticking to it

knead keep pressing and pushing dough with your hands so that it becomes very soft and stretchy

melt change from solid to liquid when heated

mince squash and chop something so that it becomes a paste

ovenproof will not be cracked by the heat of an oven

paste thick mixture

peel remove the skin of a fruit or vegetable; or the skin itself (also known as rind or zest)

preheat turn the oven or grill on in advance, so that it is hot when you are ready to heat food

purée mash, sieve or blend food until it is smooth; or the blended food itself

rinse wash under a cold tap

season give extra flavour to food by adding salt or pepper

shortcrust kind of pastry with a cooked texture like a biscuit

sift shake flour or other powder through a sieve

simmer boil gently

slice cut something into thin, flat pieces

soy sauce sauce made from fermented soy beans. A popular ingredient in Chinese cooking.

sprinkle scatter small pieces or drops on to something

steam cook in steam from boiling water

stigma part of the inside of a flower that picks up pollen. Once pollen is collected on a plant's stigma, the plant can form a seed.

tender soft, but not squashy

tepid only slightly warm, lukewarm

well dip made in the centre of flour in a bowl, into which you may pour water, milk or eggs

whisk beat an ingredient, such as cream, to make it light and airy

yeast substance used to make bread rise

Index